HISTORY OF HOLIDAYS AND FESTIVALS

CHINESE NEW YEAR

BY JEAN KUO LEE

CONTENT CONSULTANT
Jonathan H. X. Lee, PhD
Professor, Asian American Studies Department
San Francisco State University

Cover image: In London, United Kingdom, people celebrate Chinese New Year with an annual parade.

Core Library
An Imprint of Abdo Publishing
abdobooks.com

abdobooks.com

Printed in the United States of America, North Mankato, Minnesota.
102023
012024

THIS BOOK CONTAINS RECYCLED MATERIALS

Cover Photo: Prisma by Dukas/Universal Images Group/Getty Images
Interior Photos: VCG/Getty Images, 4–5; SOPA Images/SIPA USA/AP Images, 7; Andrea Renault/AFP/Getty Images, 9; Shutterstock Images, 12–13, 17, 37 (noodles, hongbao, firecrackers, offerings, lantern), 37 (cleaning), 37 (clock, working), 37 (decorating, visiting friends, rice balls, fireworks), 37 (shopping); Wang Gang/FeatureChina/AP Images, 16, 43; Yao Wen-han/National Palace Museum, 20; Ton Koene/VWPics/AP Images, 22–23; Pictures From History/Universal Images Group/Getty Images, 25; TPG/cnsphotos/TopPhoto/AP Images, 27; Alessandro Bremec/NurPhoto/AP Images, 29; CFOTO/Future Publishing/Getty Images, 32–33; Santiago Mejia/San Francisco Chronicle/AP Images, 35, 45; Yang Dong/VCG/Getty Images, 38; Craig Ferguson/LightRocket/Getty Images, 40

Editor: Laura Stickney
Series Designer: Ryan Gale

Library of Congress Control Number: 2023939651

Publisher's Cataloging-in-Publication Data

Names: Lee, Jean Kuo, author.
Title: Chinese New Year / by Jean Kuo Lee
Description: Minneapolis, Minnesota: Abdo Publishing, 2024 | Series: History of holidays and festivals | Includes online resources and index.
Identifiers: ISBN 9781098292577 (lib. bdg.) | ISBN 9798384910510 (ebook)
Subjects: LCSH: Holidays--Juvenile literature. | Festivals--Juvenile literature. | Chinese New Year--Juvenile literature. | Chinese Americans--Juvenile literature.
Classification: DDC 394.261--dc23

CONTENTS

CHAPTER ONE

CELEBRATING CHINESE NEW YEAR

It is late January, and Chinese Americans are preparing to celebrate the New Year for a second time. It is the eve of Chinese New Year. To prepare, people sweep every corner of their homes and scrub every surface until it sparkles. Sporting new outfits and haircuts, people gather for family reunion dinners. Grandparents, aunts, uncles, parents, and children are all there. On the dinner menu is a whole chicken, complete with head and feet. This unbroken chicken symbolizes how

Chinese New Year reunion dinners often feature a variety of foods, such as dumplings, chicken and seafood dishes, soups, vegetables, and noodles.

PERSPECTIVES

FIRECRACKERS

One Chinese New Year tradition involves lighting small red firecrackers. Chinese American Meiwen Chang recalls how special this tradition was when she was growing up in Taiwan. Kids were allowed to set off firecrackers during the day. "It was the only time of the year we got to light firecrackers," she said. "The kids would use an incense stick to light the wick of a single red firecracker." Chang also remembers how people in her neighborhood would go outside at midnight on New Year's Eve to light spectacular firecrackers. These were strung on a rope hung from a tall pole or the eaves of a building. Once lit, the firecrackers exploded, creating tremendous noise.

the family will stay together. Adults give eager children red envelopes filled with money. On this night, some families also pay respect to their ancestors through food offerings at the family shrine.

The next day is New Year's Day. To celebrate, some people enjoy a Chinese New Year parade with loud drums, cymbals, and firecrackers. Lion dance and dragon dance performances remind Chinese Americans of

Many people shop for special Chinese New Year decorations. Red lanterns, intricate paper cuttings, and banners with symbolic words and images are popular choices.

their ancient heritage. Chinese communities worldwide wish each other a happy and prosperous New Year. In Mandarin, the language spoken in mainland China, people wish each other "*Xīn nián kuài lè*!" This means "Happy New Year!" In Cantonese, the language spoken in the southern provinces of China, people say "*Gong hei fat choy*!" This means "Wishing you happiness and prosperity!"

Homes and businesses hang bright red banners with well-wishes printed on them. The color red is everywhere, from decorations and stationery to clothing and food. This is the way Chinese communities celebrate Chinese New Year in the United States, mainland China, and places such as Hong Kong, Taiwan, Singapore, and Malaysia.

GREGORIAN NEW YEAR

The modern Western calendar is called the Gregorian calendar. Pope Gregory XIII established it in 1582. The Gregorian calendar counts January 1 as the beginning of the year. Today, most countries use this calendar. In 1923, Greece became the last country in Europe to adopt it. During the 1900s, most non-Western countries adopted the Gregorian calendar for business purposes. China adopted it in 1912 for business purposes, but the country still uses the lunar calendar to mark festivals.

AN OLD AND WIDESPREAD TRADITION

Chinese Americans are the largest Asian group in the United States.

Many cities around the world, such as New York City, hold Chinese New Year parades. These events often feature musicians, dancers, and performers wearing brightly colored traditional clothing.

Many immigrated from mainland China and Taiwan, bringing their traditions with them. In 2021, about 5.2 million Chinese Americans were living in the United States. Many cities hold public Chinese New Year celebrations in Chinese American communities across the country.

Chinese New Year falls on a different date every year. It is usually celebrated sometime between January 21 and February 20. The date of the holiday changes because it is based on a lunisolar calendar. Holidays that depend partly on a lunar calendar will have a date that changes every year. Chinese New Year is a Lunar New Year because it uses the movements of the moon to mark its date. In this way, it is similar to Easter, a Christian holiday that also depends on the lunisolar calendar. There are many other countries and cultures that celebrate their own Lunar New Years too.

Nearly one-fifth of the world's population celebrates Chinese New Year. This includes about 1.4 billion people in China as well as people in other countries. In these countries, the holiday is much longer than one day. It is a holiday season that lasts at least 15 days. In the past, the Chinese New Year holiday season could last one to two months. This is because there were several historical festivals that occurred one after another. Over thousands of years, these festivals evolved into the modern Chinese New Year that people celebrate today.

STRAIGHT TO THE SOURCE

Grace Young is an award-winning food historian who writes cookbooks featuring Chinese American cuisine. In her cookbook *The Wisdom of the Chinese Kitchen*, Young shares her family's tradition of giving *lysee*, the Cantonese name for red envelopes, on Chinese New Year:

> *Even today, when I visit my parents at Chinese New Year's I awake on New Year's morning to find two tangerines, two oranges, and a pair of lucky money envelopes, lysee, by my pillow—all auspicious symbols of good luck. As a child, I could anticipate finding these as dependably as I could a gift from the tooth fairy when I lost a tooth. Lysee are beautiful small red envelopes with money tucked inside, given to children and family members by elders.*

Source: Grace Young. *The Wisdom of the Chinese Kitchen.* Simon and Schuster, 1999, p. 123.

WHAT'S THE BIG IDEA?

Take a close look at this passage. What traditions were important to Young's family during Chinese New Year? Explain your answer by finding two or three supporting details from the passage.

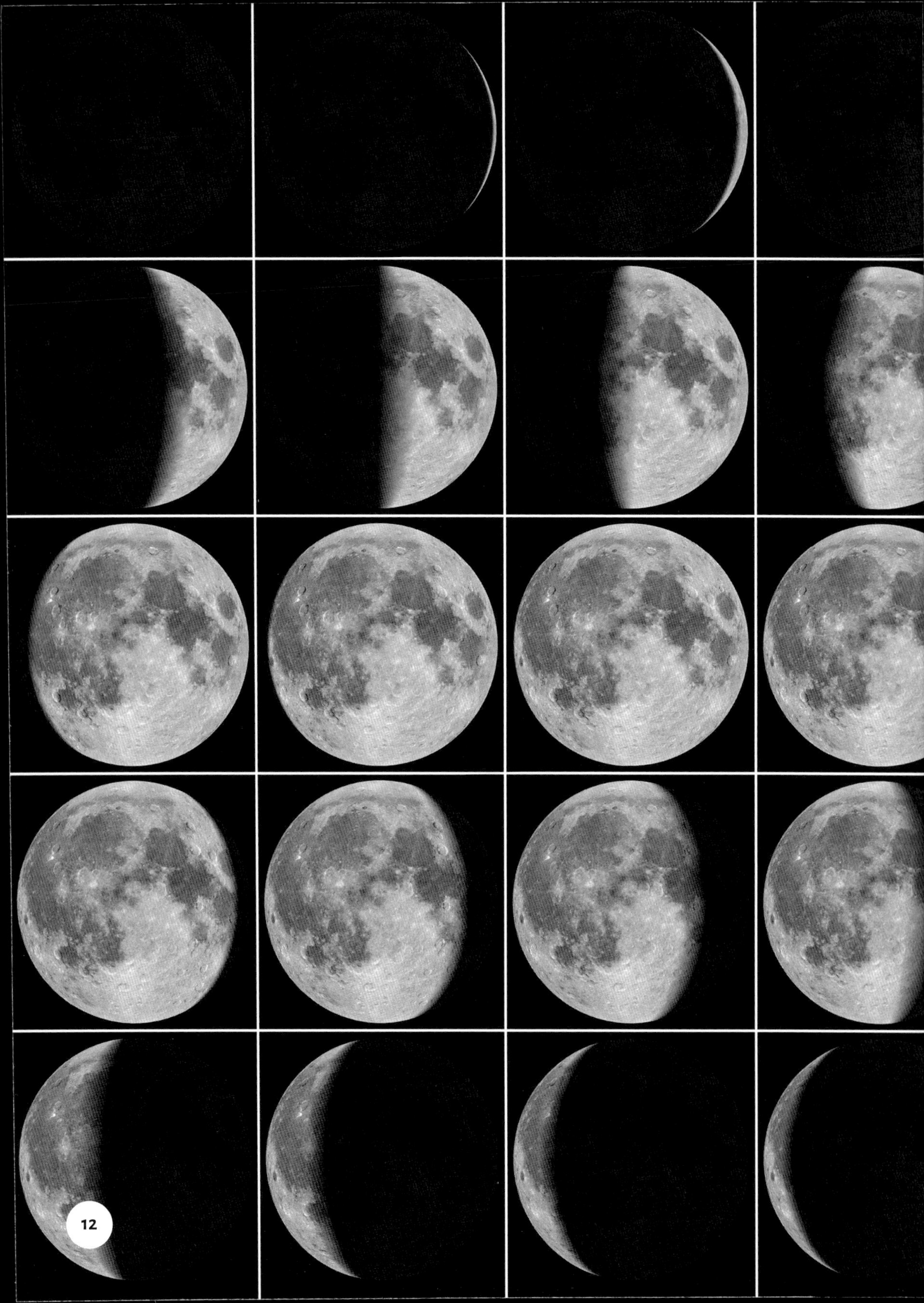

CHAPTER TWO

THE CHINESE CALENDAR

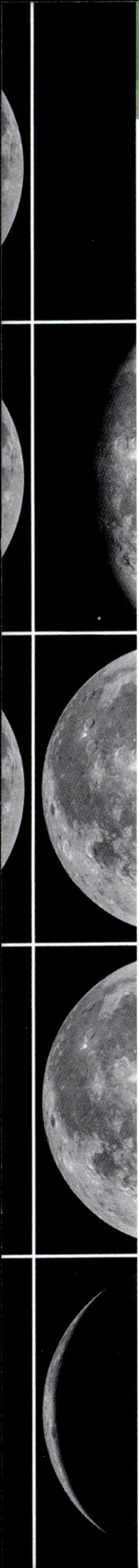

Many ancient cultures used the phases of the moon to measure time. The word *month* comes from the Old English word for moon. A month originally measured the time between two new moons. The ancient Sumerians in Mesopotamia, a region in what is now Iraq, based their calendar on the moon. The early Romans, who lived near the Mediterranean Sea, had a similar calendar. So did the Jews, Muslims, and Chinese.

Chinese New Year begins on a new moon, *top left*, when the moon is almost invisible in the sky. It ends 15 days later on a full moon, *middle row, third from left*.

The moon is central to establishing the dates for traditional Chinese festivals. Historians believe that people in China were using the moon to track time by the mid-2000s BCE. Legend says the lunar calendar has been in place since the reign of the Yellow Emperor in 2697 BCE. Chinese farmers relied on it to tell time. If they waited too long to plant a crop, they would miss the spring rains. If they did not harvest their crops on time, they might lose them to the first frost. For thousands of years, farmers

MOON PHASES

Anybody can keep track of time by observing the phases of the moon. When the moon is nearly invisible in the sky, it is called a new moon. In a lunar calendar, the time of a new moon is considered the first day of the month. A few days later, the moon's appearance grows into a crescent shape. It waxes into a half moon and then eventually into a full moon by the fifteenth day. Then the moon reverses its appearance, shrinking until it wanes into a sliver. At around 29 and a half days, it disappears to become a new moon again. The phase cycle starts over.

used moon phases to track the best times for planting and harvesting.

Telling time by observing the moon was easy. But the lunar months did not line up with the solar cycle. It takes about 365 days for Earth to make one turn around the sun. During this turn, Earth experiences the seasons of spring, summer, fall, and winter. The 12 lunar months added up to only 354 days. The difference in the cycle of months and the cycle of a year was troubling. It made the farmer's lunar calendar inaccurate when predicting seasonal changes. The same date on a lunar calendar would fall at a different seasonal time each year. This is why Chinese New Year falls on a different date every year.

THE LUNISOLAR CALENDAR

Since the Shang dynasty (1600–1050 BCE), the Chinese have used a solar calendar alongside the lunar calendar. They divided the solar year into 24 periods of time. Each period started at precisely the same time every

Modern Chinese New Year celebrations often involve merchandise and decorations that feature the year's zodiac animal. In 2022, a giant tiger lantern was displayed in Shanghai, China, to celebrate the Year of the Tiger.

year and had specific names. For example, "Beginning of Spring" began on what is February 5 in the Gregorian calendar. "Winter's Beginning" started on November 8. The solar calendar system helped farmers keep accurate agricultural dates.

THE CHINESE ZODIAC

The Chinese zodiac includes 12 different animals. People can use the solar animal cycle to find the date and animal name of each year. For example, 2024 is the Year of the Dragon. Why do you think these types of animals were chosen for the zodiac?

To keep track of solar years, the Chinese used animal names to help farmers know what year it was. There were 12 animal names for a cycle of 12 years.

during the La Festival. This celebration had grown in importance by the 600s BCE. People honored their ancestors with sacrifices of food. They also rested from farm work to enjoy feasting with their families. This took place over the course of several weeks during the twelfth lunar month. Over time, these various beginnings of the year melded together.

EXPLORE ONLINE

Chapter Two discusses the Chinese calendar and the date of Chinese New Year. The website below also talks about the date of Chinese New Year. How is the information from the website the same as the information in Chapter Two? What new information did you learn from the website?

CHINESE NEW YEAR

abdocorelibrary.com/chinese-new-year

Many artists have depicted early Chinese New Year celebrations in paintings. One painting from the Qing dynasty shows a large family celebrating the holiday with firecrackers, food, and lanterns.

覌世音

CHAPTER THREE

THE ORIGINS OF CHINESE NEW YEAR CUSTOMS

The Chinese celebrate the New Year with many traditions. These practices developed over thousands of years. Some customs have been in place since at least the 600s BCE. One such custom is offering food on an altar before a family feast. This was one of many rituals that originated from the La Festival. It gave people a way to express devotion to their families, ancestors, and gods.

Many people leave New Year offerings on their family altars. They burn incense in front of the family's ancestral tablets.

Many modern Chinese New Year customs grew out of La Festival customs.

The Chinese practiced ancestral worship. This means they honored their ancestors. During the coldest season of the year, people shared food with departed family members. They offered their ancestors a portion of cooked food on the family altar, a table on which offerings were made before the family's ancestral tablets. The names of deceased family members were written on these wooden tablets. People may have offered foods such as mutton, a type of meat that comes from sheep, and winter wine spiced with pepper. The offerings would be made during the darkest winter month, which the Chinese called the "Bitter Moon."

The Chinese also believed in household gods. These gods watched over the front door and the kitchen stove. It was common for families to offer sweets to the Kitchen God, a figure who sat in a niche or shelf above the stove. It was believed that the Kitchen God saw and heard everything. He spent the whole year with the

The Kitchen God is also known as the Stove God. It was traditional to smear honey on the Kitchen God's lips so that he would have only sweet words to say in his report to the Jade Emperor.

family, so he was believed to report on their behavior. According to Chinese folk religion, the Kitchen God visited the Jade Emperor, the highest god, just before the New Year. He delivered a report on the words and actions of family members in the household. People feared that a bad report would have negative effects, such as shortening a family member's life.

The Chinese have been celebrating the ancient customs of the La Festival for at least 2,500 years.

But by 1949, the Communist Party had gained power in China and established the People's Republic of China. In 1966, the country experienced what is known as the Cultural Revolution. During this period, leaders of the People's Republic of China banned old traditions, such as Chinese folk religion. This meant worshipping the Kitchen God was forbidden. Worshipping the gods of Chinese folk religion was considered an old tradition. The Communist government thought old traditions prevented the country from making progress. But in places such as Hong Kong and Taiwan, people were not part of the Cultural Revolution. They continued to practice ancient customs.

DRIVING OUT EVIL SPIRITS

Another La Festival custom is cleaning the house before the New Year. This tradition came from a La Festival ceremony called the Great Exorcism. This ritual was meant to drive out evil spirits. The Chinese believed they needed to scare away evil things to avoid diseases,

During Chinese New Year, some people perform ancient Nuo dances wearing traditional masks. These dances were originally used during exorcism rituals to drive away evil spirits.

droughts, and other disasters. During exorcism rituals, people made loud noises to scare off ghosts. They used drums and thin sticks of bamboo that would explode in fire. These bamboo sticks were early versions of firecrackers. Inside their homes, people cleaned to sweep away evil spirits.

Great Exorcism rituals were also practiced at the emperor's court during the Han dynasty. An exorcist leader wore a mask made of bearskin as he chanted and danced through the palace. More than 100 attendants followed him as they beat their drums. Some were dressed as animals to scare away evil spirits.

Over time, exorcism rituals were replaced by New Year parades and performances. Instead of holding exorcism ceremonies, performers beat drums, set off firecrackers, and danced in lion and dragon costumes. Lion dances feature acrobats dressed in long, colorful fur that shakes as they dance. Since lions are not native to China, historians believe they were introduced from Persia or India. During the Song dynasty (960–1279 CE), Chinese

THE NIAN MONSTER

An old Chinese legend describes a wild beast that appeared at the end of winter to devour villagers. People called the beast *Nian,* which means "year" in Chinese. The villagers discovered the beast was afraid of noise, bright lights, and the color red. So to chase the monster away, the villagers banged drums, lit firecrackers, and hung red decorations. The Chinese use this folktale to explain why they celebrate the New Year with firecrackers and the color red.

Modern lion dances are performed by two people inside a large, brightly colored lion costume. One person controls the lion's head, while the other controls the body. Some lion dancers perform on stilts.

armies used lion dancers to scare away the horses and elephants used by enemy armies. This custom became more popular during the Ming dynasty (1368–1644 CE). During this time, villagers used lion dances to keep predators away from their farm animals.

Dragon dances feature a line of dancers who run while covered by a long, colorful dragon costume. The dragon is one of the Chinese zodiac animals. It is a

凡人微光 汇聚成炬 中国力量 未来希望
12306
SALE
旅友书屋
RELAY
旅友书屋
Diplomat 外交官
Hisense
Hisense

CHAPTER FOUR

A MODERN FESTIVAL

Over time, people adapted ancient Chinese New Year customs to modern life. In China, the Lunar New Year is now called *Chunjie,* or Spring Festival. This is because in 1912, China adopted January 1 as the New Year. To avoid confusion, the Lunar New Year was renamed the Spring Festival. In 1949, China became a Communist country. During this shift, the Chinese government discarded the lunar calendar and Lunar New Year because they involved old customs.

In China, the Spring Festival travel season begins several weeks before the new year. During this time, train stations, airports, and tourist sites are often crowded.

It banned firecrackers, offerings to the gods, and other New Year traditions. Only private celebrations continued.

In 1996, China officially made the Spring Festival a week-long state holiday. Since the late 1900s, the government has allowed nonreligious celebrations of the festival. People usually take seven days off work and travel to their hometowns for reunion dinners. During the New Year season in China, hundreds of

A GLOBAL NEW YEAR

Chinese New Year is the celebration of the Lunar New Year in China and Chinese communities. But other East Asian countries celebrate the Lunar New Year, too. In Korea, the celebration is called Seollal. In Mongolia, it is called Tsagaan Sar. In Vietnam, people celebrate Tết. People in these countries share some New Year traditions, such as cleaning the house, honoring ancestors, and feasting with family. But each culture adds a special twist to the holiday. Koreans may dress up in traditional Korean outfits. Some Vietnamese people burn paper money for loved ones who have passed away.

The San Francisco Chinese New Year Parade attracts millions of spectators every year. It features dragon dances, colorful floats, costumes, and performers.

millions of people move by road, train, and airplane to reach home for the holidays.

There are many variations of Chinese New Year traditions too. Chinese communities may celebrate differently depending on where they live. For example, in the southern Chinese city of Hong Kong, fewer people celebrate the Lantern Festival, which marks the end of the New Year season. This is because it began as a northern Chinese tradition. Families may also celebrate different parts of the holiday season. In the United States, Chinese Americans may celebrate with only a family reunion meal on New Year's Eve. They might watch the San Francisco Chinese New Year Parade, the largest of its kind outside of Asia.

CHINESE NEW YEAR TODAY

Today, Chinese people continue to celebrate the New Year in ways that are based on ancient traditions. The holiday season lasts for several weeks. A few days before the New Year, families clean their homes. Children dust away cobwebs and polish furniture. Adults may buy new drapes, chair covers, or bed linens. It is believed that people must do these things before the New Year. If they clean their houses after the New Year begins, they believe they will "sweep away" the good fortune of the New Year. They hang New Year wishes beside doorways, too. These wishes are often printed on bright red paper. They include sayings such as "May you realize your ambitions."

THE CHINESE NEW YEAR HOLIDAY **SEASON**

This timeline shows the events of the Chinese New Year holiday season in China. Based on the information provided, how many days would you expect the Chinese New Year holiday season to last? What is the significance of each tradition and activity?

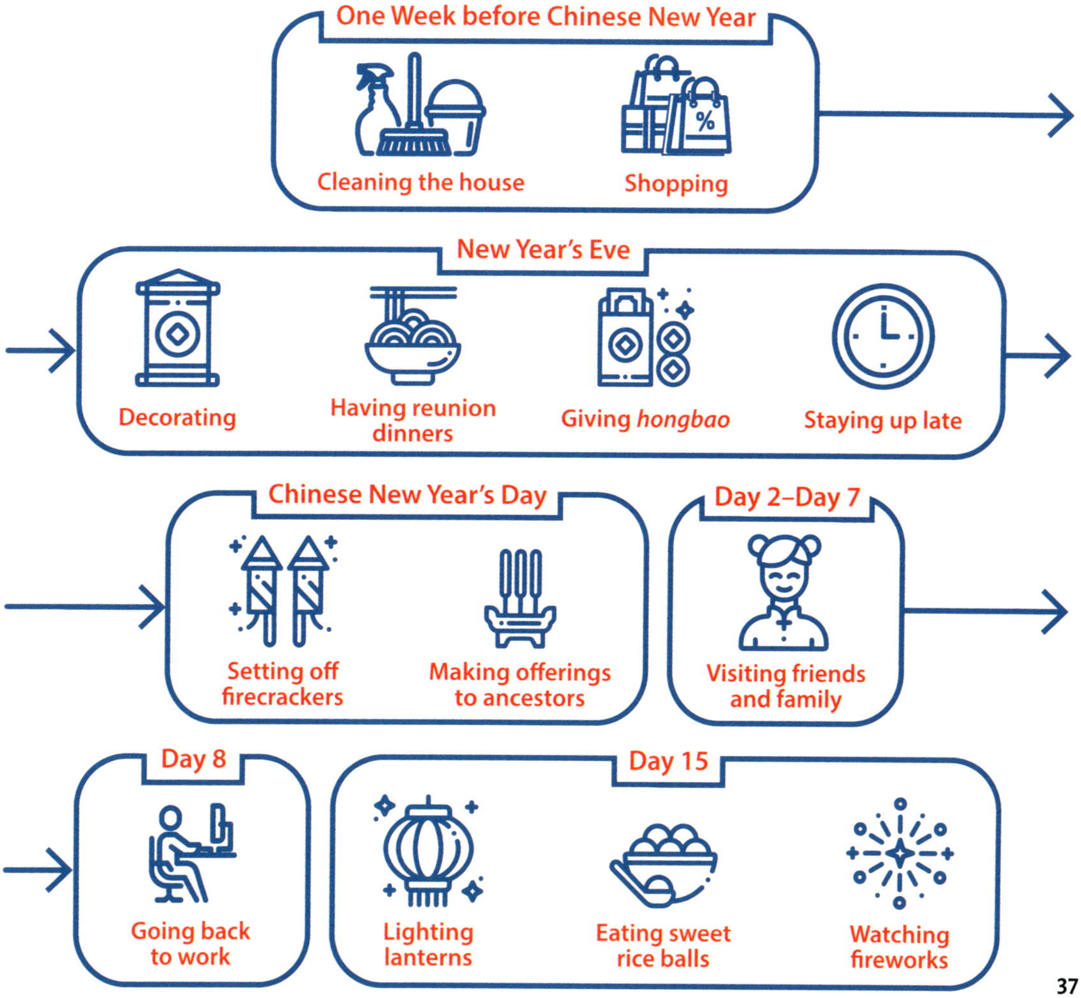

During the Lantern Festival, people light lanterns of all shapes and sizes. Some lanterns have riddles written on them, while others are shaped like lucky animals such as fish.

People may also hang symbols of wealth, such as Chinese coins. Others decorate with flowers and fruit trees. Round fruits, such as oranges, are popular because they resemble the moon.

For many families, Chinese New Year involves a lot of preparation. People must get ready for one of the biggest feasts of the year. Before the New Year, families start planning and shopping for the feast. As they prepare food in the kitchen, some people hang a slip of paper with the Kitchen God's name on it. This helps make sure the Kitchen God gives the family a good report. People must also settle all debts before the New Year. Beginning the year in debt is considered unlucky.

On New Year's Eve, family members return home for reunion dinners. They serve foods whose names have favorable double meanings. For example, *yu* means "fish" in Chinese. But it also means "abundance." Some families may serve dumplings, rice cakes, or seafood. Before eating dinner, the family may present the food to their ancestors

PERSPECTIVES

GIFT GIVING

Giving gifts during Chinese New Year is common when visiting family and friends. Some people give gifts of food. Another gift might be a tray of preserved fruits and snacks such as kumquats, red dates, and melon seeds. Flowers are a popular gift, but only if they are the right kind. A Chinese relative or friend might be offended by a gift of white flowers. Writer Rosemary Geng says this is because white "is a color of mourning." She says, "When in doubt, always give a Chinese auntie seasonal fruit, candy, or cookies when visiting."

Hongbao are often intricately decorated with golden illustrations, symbols of luck, and Chinese sayings. Some may feature the zodiac animal of the year.

and gods. Children receive *hongbao*. In return, they show respect to their parents and elders by bowing to thank them. They stay up late with the adults.

On New Year's Day, people go out to visit friends and watch performances. Parades with dragon and lion dances fill the streets. Firecrackers pop and sizzle. People pass out candies such as sugared coconut slices and sweet melon pieces. *Nian gao,* a sweet rice cake, is another popular treat. Many people take time off from work for the New Year so that they can enjoy the festivities with their friends and families.

During the next few weeks, families may visit temples to give thanks to the gods. They visit friends and dine with family members. They attend parades and street fairs. On the fifteenth day, people light red lanterns for the Lantern Festival. They eat sweet rice balls that look like the moon. The first full moon of the New Year brings the celebrations to an end.

Chinese New Year is a time to look forward to each year. People may celebrate the season differently, but the purpose of the holiday remains the same. It is a time for renewal, reconnecting with family, and wishing peace and happiness to loved ones.

FURTHER EVIDENCE

Chapter Four explores how people celebrate Chinese New Year today. What is the main point of this chapter? What key evidence supports this point? Go to the article about the Lunar New Year at the website below. Find a quote from the website that supports the chapter's main point.

LUNAR NEW YEAR

abdocorelibrary.com/chinese-new-year

IMPORTANT DATES

2697 BCE
According to legend, the first lunar calendar is created during the reign of the Yellow Emperor.

1600–1050
By the Shang dynasty, the lunar calendar becomes a lunisolar calendar.

600s
The La Festival is established as an important festival in China.

206 BCE–220 CE
The Han dynasty rules China. The emperor declares that the beginning of the year will be when the second new moon appears in the sky after the winter solstice.

1912
The Republic of China switches to the Gregorian calendar, adopting January 1 as the first day of the New Year. The Lunar New Year is renamed the Spring Festival.

1949
The Communist Party of China founds the People's Republic of China.

1966
The Cultural Revolution begins in China. The Communist Party of China sweeps through the country and bans many Lunar New Year traditions.

1996
The Chinese government loosens bans on Lunar New Year traditions. It institutes a weeklong vacation for workers to travel home for the Spring Festival.

STOP AND THINK

Tell the Tale

Chapter Four of this book discusses how people celebrate Chinese New Year. Imagine you are visiting family or friends and joining in the festivities of the season. Write 200 words about the activities you take part in.

Surprise Me

Chapter Two discusses the Chinese calendar. After reading this book, what two or three facts about the Chinese calendar did you find most surprising? Write a few sentences about each fact. Why did you find each fact surprising?

Another View

This book talks about the origins of Chinese New Year. As you know, every source is different. Ask a librarian or another adult to help you find another source about the holiday's origins. Write a short essay comparing and contrasting the new source's point of view with that of this book's author. What is the point of view of each author? How are they similar and why? How are they different and why?

Dig Deeper

After reading this book, what questions do you still have about Chinese New Year? With an adult's help, find a few reliable sources that can help you answer your questions. Write a paragraph about what you learned.

GLOSSARY

communist
relating to a system of social organization in which the workers own the means of production and there is no private property

debt
something that is owed

dynasty
a succession of rulers descended from the same ancestor

exorcism
a ceremony for getting rid of evil spirits

heritage
practices or customs handed down as a tradition

immigrate
to move to and resettle in a new country

Indigenous
relating to the earliest known inhabitants of a place

prosperous
successful and thriving

province
a district of a country

shrine
a place where people pay respects to a person or deity

solstice
the time of the year when the sun is farthest north or south from Earth's equator

ONLINE RESOURCES

To learn more about Chinese New Year, visit our free resource websites below.

Core Library CONNECTION
FREE! COMMON CORE MULTIMEDIA RESOURCES

Visit **abdocorelibrary.com** or scan this QR code for free Common Core resources for teachers and students, including vetted activities, multimedia, and booklinks, for deeper subject comprehension.

Booklinks NONFICTION NETWORK
FREE! ONLINE NONFICTION RESOURCES

Visit **abdobooklinks.com** or scan this QR code for free additional online weblinks for further learning. These links are routinely monitored and updated to provide the most current information available.

LEARN MORE

Chu, Eugenia. *Celebrating Chinese New Year.* Rockridge, 2021.

Gagne, Tammy. *Chinese Gods, Heroes, and Mythology.* Abdo, 2019.

Hwang, Aaron. *A Kid's Guide to the Chinese Zodiac.* Running, 2023.

INDEX

About the Author

Jean Kuo Lee is a Chinese American author. She loved to eat *Nian Gao* and receive hongbao as a child during Chinese New Year.